Collins

Easy Learning

Times tables Workbook 1

Age 5-7

Simon Greaves

This book belongs to

_____

How to use this book

- Easy Learning workbooks help your child improve basic skills, build confidence and develop a love of learning.
- Find a quiet, comfortable place to work, away from distractions.
- Get into a routine of completing one or two workbook pages with your child every day.
- Ask your child to circle the star that matches how many questions they have completed every two pages:

Some = half of the questions

Most = more than half

All = all the questions

- The progress certificate at the back of this book will help you and your child keep track of how many ⭐ have been circled.
- Encourage your child to work through all of the questions eventually, and praise them for completing the progress certificate.
- Each workbook builds on the previous one in the series. Help your child complete this one to ensure they have covered what they need to know before starting the next workbook.

- The ability to recall and use times tables facts is an essential skill and is invaluable for many mathematical processes.
- Learning tables at an early age gives your child confidence with numbers.

Parent tip
Look out for tips on how to help your child learn tables.

- Ask your child to find and colour the little monkeys that are hidden throughout this book.
- This will help engage them with the pages of the book and get them interested in the activities.

(Don't count this one.)

Published by Collins
An imprint of HarperCollins*Publishers*
77–85 Fulham Palace Road
Hammersmith
London
W6 8JB

Browse the complete Collins catalogue at
www.collinseducation.com

First published in 2011
© HarperCollins*Publishers* 2011

10 9 8 7 6 5 4

ISBN-13 978-0-00-727760-5

The author asserts the moral right to be identified as the author of this work.

British Library Cataloguing in Publication Data
A catalogue record for this publication is available from the British Library

Written by Simon Greaves
Design and layout by Linda Miles, Lodestone Publishing
Illustrated by Graham Smith and Jenny Tulip
Cover design by Linda Miles
Cover illustration by Graham Smith
Packaged and project managed by White-Thomson Publishing Ltd
Printed and bound in China

Contents

Two times table

1 Fill in the missing answers.

$3 \times 2 = \boxed{}$ $7 \times 2 = \boxed{}$ $5 \times 2 = \boxed{}$

$6 \times 2 = \boxed{}$ $10 \times 2 = \boxed{}$ $2 \times 2 = \boxed{}$

$4 \times 2 = \boxed{}$ $8 \times 2 = \boxed{}$ $9 \times 2 = \boxed{}$

2 Shoes come in pairs. There are two shoes in each pair.
Complete the multiplication for each picture.

$3 \times 2 = 6$

$5 \times 2 = \boxed{}$

$\boxed{} \times 2 = \boxed{}$

$\boxed{} \times 2 = \boxed{}$

3 Colour yellow all the shapes that have an answer in the two times table.
What do you see?

_____

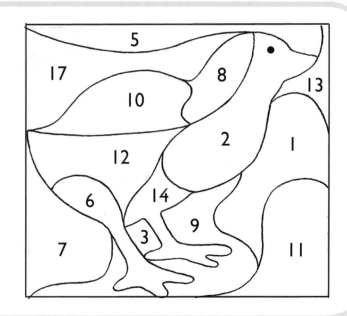

Parent tip
Sing the two times table along to the tune of a favourite song.

4

4 In each line, circle the multiplication that matches the number in the triangle.

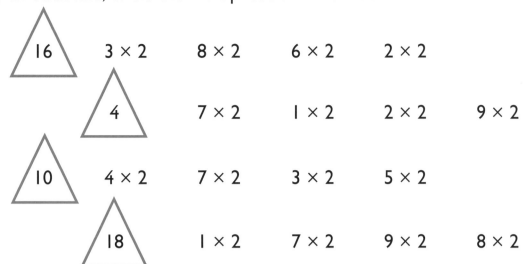

	3 × 2	8 × 2	6 × 2	2 × 2	
	7 × 2	1 × 2	2 × 2	9 × 2
	4 × 2	7 × 2	3 × 2	5 × 2	
	1 × 2	7 × 2	9 × 2	8 × 2

5 Some of these football shirts have answers in the two times table.
Colour red all of the shirts that have an answer in the two times table.
Colour blue all of the shirts that do not.

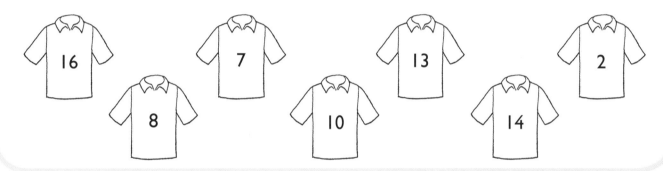

6 Here is a machine that multiplies numbers by two.
Fill in the missing numbers.

How much did you do?   Questions 1–6

Circle the star to show what you have done.

 Some

 Most

 All

5

7 Count the coins and complete each multiplication.

$3 \times 2p = 6p$

$\times 2p =$

8 Fill in the missing numbers.

$20 = \boxed{} \times 2$ $10 = \boxed{} \times 2$

$18 = \boxed{} \times 2$ $16 = \boxed{} \times 2$

$4 = \boxed{} \times 2$ $6 = \boxed{} \times 2$

$8 = \boxed{} \times 2$ $2 = \boxed{} \times 2$

Parent tip
Make a chart for your child to keep track of which twos they know/need to learn.

9 Count on or back in twos. Fill in the missing numbers.

2	4				12		
6	8					18	
20	18				10		
16				8	6		

10 Here are some multiplications. Some are correct, some are not.
Put a tick next to those with the correct answer. ✔
Put a cross next to those with the wrong answer. ✘

2 × 2 = 4 ☐   9 × 2 = 18 ☐

6 × 2 = 14 ☐   5 × 2 = 12 ☐

7 × 2 = 18 ☐   10 × 2 = 20 ☐

4 × 2 = 10 ☐   3 × 2 = 6 ☐

11 Colour a path through the number grid. You must only go through answers that are in the two times table.

21	3	23	7	18	→ Finish
5	7	9	10	14	
1	11	13	6	25	
19	8	20	12	3	
16	4	5	17	27	
2	1	13	15	29	

Start → (points to 2)

12 Draw a line to join each multiplication to its answer.

4 × 2   6 × 2   9 × 2   2 × 2   3 × 2   10 × 2

(18)   (6)   (8)   (12)   (20)   (4)

How much did you do?   Questions 7–12

Circle the star
to show what
you have done.

Some

Most

All

Ten times table

The ten times table tells you how to count in sets of ten.

1 Fill in the missing answers.

$3 \times 10 =$ ☐ $6 \times 10 =$ ☐ $5 \times 10 =$ ☐

$9 \times 10 =$ ☐ $7 \times 10 =$ ☐ $8 \times 10 =$ ☐

$10 \times 10 =$ ☐ $2 \times 10 =$ ☐ $4 \times 10 =$ ☐

2 Find the total in each money box.

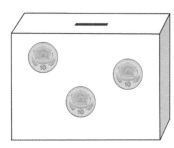

$3 \times 10p =$

$8 \times \quad p =$

$\quad \times \quad p =$

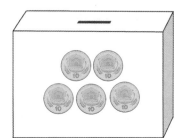

3 Draw a line to join each multiplication to its answer.

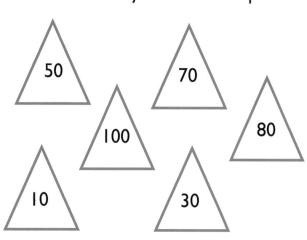

50   70   100   80   10   30

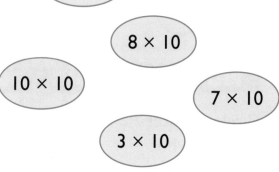

5×10 1×10 8×10 10×10 7×10 3×10

4 Here is a machine that multiplies numbers by ten. Fill in the missing numbers.

3 → [ ] → [ ]
8 → [ ] → [ ]
9 → × 10 → [ ]
6 → [ ] → [ ]

5 Count on or back in tens. Fill in the missing numbers.

10	[ ]	30	[ ]	[ ]	[ ]	[ ]
100	[ ]	[ ]	70	[ ]	[ ]	[ ]
40	[ ]	[ ]	[ ]	[ ]	90	[ ]
70	[ ]	50	[ ]	[ ]	[ ]	[ ]

Parent tip
Chant the answers to the ten times table forwards and backwards.

6 A jar contains ten sweets.

How many sweets in 3 jars?   3 × 10 = 30

How many sweets in 5 jars?   5 × [ ] = [ ]

How many sweets in 7 jars?   [ ] × 10 = [ ]

How many sweets in 9 jars?   [ ] × [ ] = [ ]

How many sweets in 10 jars?   [ ] × [ ] = [ ]

How much did you do?   Questions 1–6

Circle the star to show what you have done.

 Some    Most   All

7 Here are some objects on a shelf.
Find the number on each object then complete the multiplication.

hat	☐	=	☐	× 10
bucket	☐	=	☐	× 10
football	☐	=	☐	× 10
bell	☐	=	☐	× 10
cup	☐	=	☐	× 10
book	☐	=	☐	× 10
clock	☐	=	☐	× 10

8 Circle the numbers that are answers in the ten times table.

38   70   25   50   100   40   88   22   45   20

9 Complete these multiplications.

4 × 10 = ☐   9 × ☐ = 90

☐ × 10 = 70   10 × ☐ = 100

6 × ☐ = 60   ☐ × 10 = 30

5 × 10 = ☐   2 × 10 = ☐

☐ × 10 = 10   ☐ × 10 = 80

Parent tip
Look for answers in the ten times table on everyday objects.

10

10 Colour red all the shapes that have an answer in the ten times table. What do you see?

_____

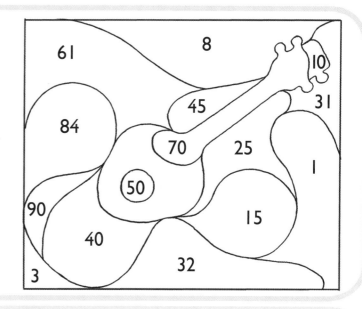

11 Here are some multiplications. Some are correct and some are not.
Put a tick next to those with the correct answer. ✔
Put a cross next to those with the wrong answer. ✘

$2 \times 10 = 20$ ☐ $8 \times 10 = 100$ ☐ $5 \times 10 = 60$ ☐

$9 \times 10 = 90$ ☐ $4 \times 10 = 40$ ☐ $7 \times 10 = 50$ ☐

$3 \times 10 = 10$ ☐ $6 \times 10 = 60$ ☐ $10 \times 10 = 100$ ☐

12 So you think you know the ten times table?
Write out the full table below.

☐ × ☐ = ☐   ☐ × ☐ = ☐

☐ × ☐ = ☐   ☐ × ☐ = ☐

☐ × ☐ = ☐   ☐ × ☐ = ☐

☐ × ☐ = ☐   ☐ × ☐ = ☐

☐ × ☐ = ☐   ☐ × ☐ = ☐

How much did you do?   ## Questions 7–12

Circle the star
to show what
you have done.

Some

Most

All

Mixed tables

1 Fill in the missing answers.

$2 \times 2 = \boxed{}$ $7 \times 2 = \boxed{}$ $6 \times 2 = \boxed{}$ $1 \times 10 = \boxed{}$

$3 \times 10 = \boxed{}$ $9 \times 2 = \boxed{}$ $10 \times 10 = \boxed{}$ $8 \times 2 = \boxed{}$

$6 \times 10 = \boxed{}$ $3 \times 2 = \boxed{}$ $5 \times 10 = \boxed{}$ $2 \times 10 = \boxed{}$

$1 \times 2 = \boxed{}$ $4 \times 2 = \boxed{}$ $5 \times 2 = \boxed{}$ $7 \times 10 = \boxed{}$

$10 \times 2 = \boxed{}$ $8 \times 10 = \boxed{}$ $4 \times 10 = \boxed{}$ $9 \times 10 = \boxed{}$

2 Complete the multiplication grid.

×	3	6	9	10	7
2					
10					

Parent tip
Remember to ask your child to find and colour the monkey.

3 Look at the numbers in the box below.

2	13	18
17	10	
4	12	8
20	15	19

Circle in green any number that is an answer in the two times table.

Circle in red any number that is an answer in the ten times table.

Which two numbers are answers in both the two and ten times tables?

$\boxed{}$ $\boxed{}$

4 Write a multiplication to show the number of gloves in each group.
Write another multiplication to show the number of fingers on the gloves in each group.

$2 \times 2 = 4$ gloves
$2 \times 10 = 20$ fingers

☐ $\times\ 2\ =$ ☐   gloves

☐ $\times\ 10\ =$ ☐   fingers

☐ $\times\ 2\ =$ ☐   gloves

☐ $\times\ 10\ =$ ☐   fingers

☐ $\times\ 2\ =$ ☐   gloves

☐ $\times\ 10\ =$ ☐   fingers

5 Here are some balloons.
Colour the balloons that have an answer in the two or ten times tables.
Use a different colour for each balloon.

8   16   13

19

21   17   20   2   100   40

6 Draw a line to join each multiplication to its answer.

10×2 8×2 9×10 7×2 3×10 5×10

(90)   (30)   (14)   (50)   (20)   (16)

How much did you do?   Questions 1–6

Circle the star to show what you have done.

 Some

 Most

 All

7 Find the multiplication for each shape and complete the missing tables facts.

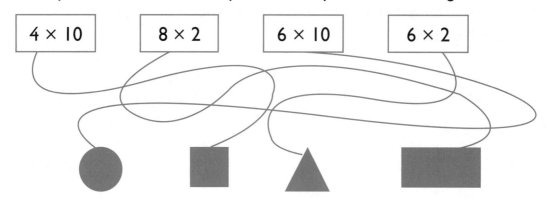

| 4 × 10 | 8 × 2 | 6 × 10 | 6 × 2 |

circle ☐ × ☐ = ☐   square ☐ × ☐ = ☐

triangle ☐ × ☐ = ☐   rectangle ☐ × ☐ = ☐

8 Here are the prices of two items in a shop. How much will it cost to buy the following items?

6 pencils ☐ p   3 notebooks ☐ p

4 pencils ☐ p   5 notebooks ☐ p

8 pencils ☐ p   7 notebooks ☐ p

10p

2p

9 Work out the answer to each multiplication on the clown's face. Use the answers to find the correct colour in the code key. Colour the picture.

Code key
8 = pink
10 = yellow
14 = blue
18 = green
20 = red
40 = purple

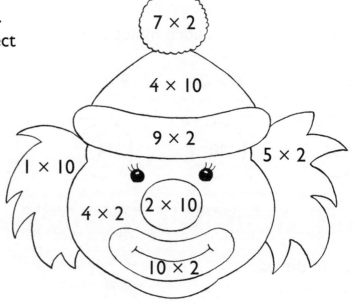

7 × 2
4 × 10
9 × 2
1 × 10
5 × 2
4 × 2
2 × 10
10 × 2

Parent tip
Record the ten times table on a media player for your child to listen to and write down.

10 Count on or back in twos or tens. Fill in the missing numbers.

2	☐	☐	8	☐	☐	☐
90	☐	70	☐	☐	☐	☐
20	☐	16	☐	☐	☐	☐
40	☐	☐	70	☐	☐	☐

11 Find a way along the road from the start to the finish. You must only go through answers that are in the two or ten times tables.

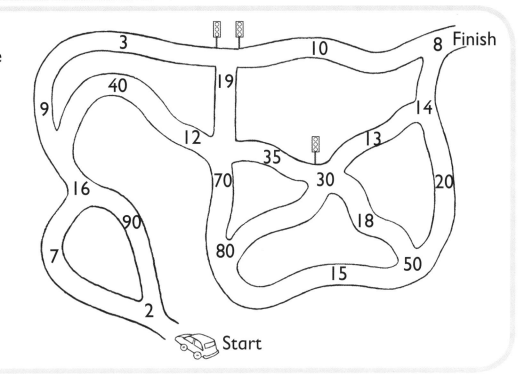

12 Write in the missing numbers to complete each multiplication.

☐ × 2 = 12   7 × ☐ = 14

8 × ☐ = 80   ☐ × 10 = 60

☐ × 2 = 20   5 × ☐ = 50

10 × ☐ = 100   ☐ × 2 = 8

Five times table

1 Fill in the missing answers.

3 × 5 = ☐   10 × 5 = ☐   5 × 5 = ☐

6 × 5 = ☐   7 × 5 = ☐   9 × 5 = ☐

4 × 5 = ☐   8 × 5 = ☐   2 × 5 = ☐

2 Start from 5 and count on in fives, joining the dots as you go. What do you see?

_____

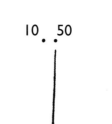

30   35
25
20   40
15   10 50   45

5

Parent tip
Recite the five times table backwards with your child.

3 Draw lines to join each key to the correct door.

 45
 15
 35
 25
50

 10 × 5   3 × 5

 5 × 5

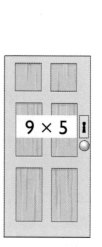 9 × 5

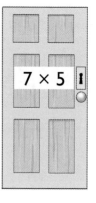 7 × 5

4 In each line, circle the multiplication that matches the number in the box.

20	3 × 5	4 × 5	6 × 5	2 × 5
35	7 × 5	3 × 5	2 × 5	9 × 5
15	4 × 5	7 × 5	3 × 5	5 × 5
40	10 × 5	7 × 5	9 × 5	8 × 5

5 Draw coins to show the amount in each money box.

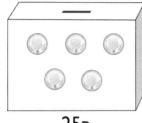

25p

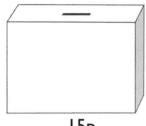

15p

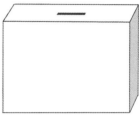

40p

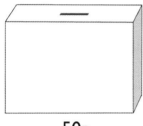

50p

10p

35p

6 Here are some multiplications. Some are correct and some are not.
Put a tick next to those with the correct answer.   ✔
Put a cross next to those with the wrong answer.   ✗

3 × 5 = 15 ☐   8 × 5 = 40 ☐   6 × 5 = 25 ☐

9 × 5 = 45 ☐   2 × 5 = 10 ☐   1 × 5 = 10 ☐

10 × 5 = 45 ☐   4 × 5 = 25 ☐   7 × 5 = 35 ☐

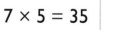

7 Count on or back in fives. Fill in the missing numbers.

5	□	□	20	□	□	□
45	□	35	□	□	□	□
15	□	□	□	35	□	□
35	□	□	□	□	10	□

8 Colour the squares that have answers in the five times table.
Spot the pattern.

1	2	3	4	5	6	7	8	9	10
11	12	13	14	15	16	17	18	19	20
21	22	23	24	25	26	27	28	29	30
31	32	33	34	35	36	37	38	39	40
41	42	43	44	45	46	47	48	49	50

9 The ship needs to reach the harbour. It must follow a route that only has answers to the five times table. Colour the route the ship must take.

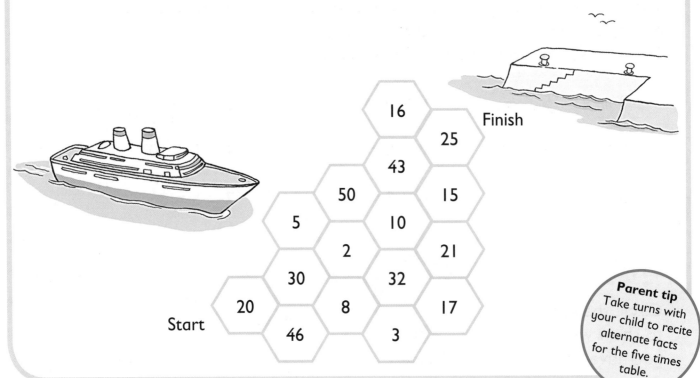

16
25
Finish
43
50 15
5 10
2 21
30 32
20 8 17
Start
46 3

Parent tip
Take turns with your child to recite alternate facts for the five times table.

10 The castle holds the answers to the five times table. Find the answer on each part of the castle and then complete the multiplication.

door   ☐ = ☐ × 5

moat   ☐ = ☐ × 5

window   ☐ = ☐ × 5

flag   ☐ = ☐ × 5

drawbridge   ☐ = ☐ × 5

wall   ☐ = ☐ × 5

tower   ☐ = ☐ × 5

11 Fill in the missing numbers for these five times table facts.

☐ × 5 = 45   6 × 5 = ☐

10 = ☐ × 5   8 × 5 = ☐

20 = ☐ × 5   50 = ☐ × 5

12 So you think you know the five times table?
Write out the full table below.

☐ × ☐ = ☐   ☐ × ☐ = ☐

☐ × ☐ = ☐   ☐ × ☐ = ☐

☐ × ☐ = ☐   ☐ × ☐ = ☐

☐ × ☐ = ☐   ☐ × ☐ = ☐

☐ × ☐ = ☐   ☐ × ☐ = ☐

How much did you do?   Questions 7–12

Circle the star to show what you have done.

 Some

 Most

 All

Mixed tables

1 Write in the missing answers.

2 × 5 = ☐   8 × 10 = ☐   1 × 5 = ☐   8 × 5 = ☐

1 × 10 = ☐   7 × 5 = ☐   7 × 10 = ☐   4 × 10 = ☐

3 × 10 = ☐   6 × 10 = ☐   10 × 5 = ☐   9 × 5 = ☐

3 × 5 = ☐   10 × 10 = ☐   2 × 10 = ☐   5 × 5 = ☐

5 × 10 = ☐   4 × 5 = ☐   6 × 5 = ☐   9 × 10 = ☐

2 Draw lines to match the multiplications that have the same answers.

(2 × 5)   (6 × 5)   (4 × 5)   (10 × 5)   (8 × 5)

[3 × 10]   [5 × 10]   [2 × 10]   [4 × 10]   [1 × 10]

3 Each shape has an answer to either the five or the ten times table.
Find the answer on each shape and then complete the multiplication.

triangle   ☐ = ☐ × 10

square   ☐ = ☐ × 10

circle   ☐ = ☐ × 5

oval   ☐ = ☐ × 5

diamond   ☐ = ☐ × 10

rectangle   ☐ = ☐ × 5

25   100   15   80   60   45

4 Work out the total amount of money in each purse.

[ ] × 5p = [ ] p

[ ] × [ ] p = [ ] p

[ ] × [ ] p = [ ] p

[ ] × [ ] p = [ ] p

[ ] × [ ] p = [ ] p

5 Here are some multiplications. Some are correct and some are not.
Put a tick next to those with the correct answer. ✔
Put a cross next to those with the wrong answer. ✗

$2 \times 10 = 20$ [ ] $5 \times 5 = 30$ [ ] $10 \times 10 = 90$ [ ]

$7 \times 5 = 35$ [ ] $6 \times 10 = 60$ [ ] $4 \times 5 = 25$ [ ]

$4 \times 10 = 50$ [ ] $9 \times 5 = 45$ [ ] $6 \times 5 = 40$ [ ]

6 Fill in the missing numbers by counting on or back in fives or tens.

5	10	[ ]	[ ]	[ ]	30	[ ]
15	[ ]	25	[ ]	[ ]	40	[ ]
45	[ ]	[ ]	[ ]	[ ]	20	[ ]
70	[ ]	[ ]	[ ]	30	[ ]	[ ]
10	[ ]	[ ]	40	[ ]	[ ]	[ ]

Parent tip
Make flash cards of the five and ten times tables to test your child.

How much did you do?   Questions 1–6

Circle the star
to show what
you have done.

 Some

 Most

 All

7 Here are some number machines that multiply numbers by five or by ten. Write in the missing numbers.

6 →		→	
3 →	× 10	→	
5 →		→	
9 →		→	

1 →		→	
9 →	× 5	→	
5 →		→	
7 →		→	

8 Colour the squares that have answers to the five and ten times tables.
Which letter of the alphabet can you see?

_____

Parent tip
Make a poster of the five and ten times tables to stick on the wall.

10	5	25
42	100	6
38	50	56
18	15	82
80	35	45

9 Try to answer all these questions in less than two minutes. Time yourself!

5 × 5 = ☐   4 × 5 = ☐

35 = ☐ × ☐   5 = ☐ × ☐

1 × 10 = ☐   50 = ☐ × ☐

6 × 5 = ☐   7 × 10 = ☐

100 = ☐ × ☐   25 = ☐ × ☐

10 Complete the multiplication grid.

×	2	5	7	10	8
5					
10					

11 Colour red all the shapes that have an answer in the five or ten times tables. What do you see?

_____

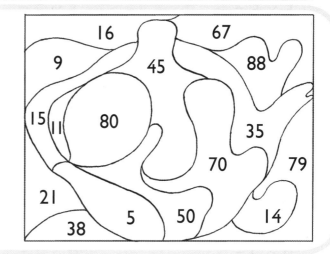

12 Fill in the missing numbers to complete the 'big ten'.

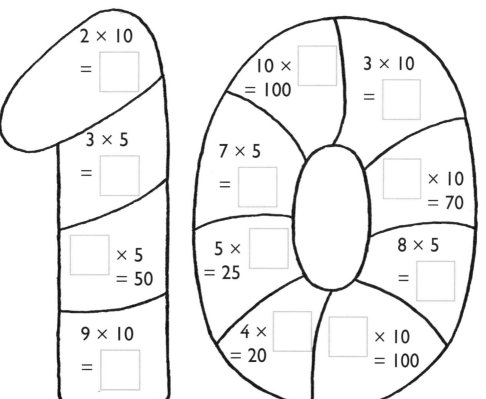

Mixed tables

1 Fill in the answers to these multiplications.

3 × 2 = ☐   3 × 5 = ☐   1 × 2 = ☐

5 × 5 = ☐   1 × 5 = ☐   10 × 5 = ☐

4 × 5 = ☐   5 × 2 = ☐   7 × 5 = ☐

8 × 2 = ☐   7 × 2 = ☐   2 × 5 = ☐

4 × 2 = ☐   10 × 2 = ☐   9 × 2 = ☐

6 × 2 = ☐   9 × 5 = ☐   2 × 2 = ☐

6 × 5 = ☐   8 × 5 = ☐   2 × 10 = ☐

2 Draw a line to join each multiplication to its answer.

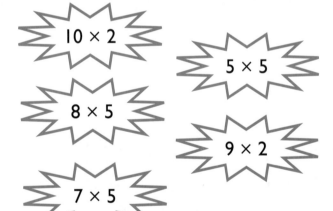
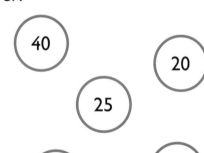

10 × 2   5 × 5   8 × 5   9 × 2   7 × 5

40   20   25   35   18

3 Fill in the missing numbers.

25 = ☐ × 5   10 = ☐ × 2

☐ = 2 × 5   ☐ = 8 × 2

40 = ☐ × 5   20 = ☐ × 2

☐ = 4 × 5   ☐ = 3 × 2

Parent tip
Recite the two and five times tables out loud.

4 Colour the fish that have answers in the two or five times tables.

5 So you think you know the two times table?
Write out the full table below.

☐ × ☐ = ☐   ☐ × ☐ = ☐

☐ × ☐ = ☐   ☐ × ☐ = ☐

☐ × ☐ = ☐   ☐ × ☐ = ☐

☐ × ☐ = ☐   ☐ × ☐ = ☐

☐ × ☐ = ☐   ☐ × ☐ = ☐

6 Write a multiplication to show the total amount of money in each of the groups below.

4 × 2p = 8p

☐ × 2p = ☐ p

☐ × 5p = ☐ p

☐ × ☐ p = ☐ p

☐ × ☐ p = ☐ p

7 Here are some targets. The arrow scores five times the number it lands on. Work out the score for each target.

 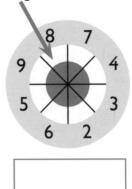 

| 6 × 5 = | | |

The arrow scores two times the number it lands on.
Work out the score for each target.

| 7 × 2 = | | |

8 Here are some multiplications. Some are correct and some are not.
Put a tick next to those with the correct answer. ✔
Put a cross next to those with the wrong answer. ✘

3 × 5 = 15 ☐   9 × 2 = 16 ☐   8 × 2 = 12 ☐

3 × 2 = 8 ☐   6 × 5 = 30 ☐   4 × 5 = 25 ☐

10 × 2 = 20 ☐   9 × 5 = 45 ☐   4 × 2 = 10 ☐

9 Draw a line to match each cup to the correct saucer.

  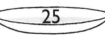

10 Here are the prices of two items in a shop.
How much will it cost to buy the following items?

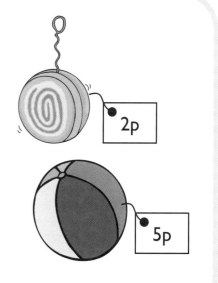

6 yo-yos ☐ p   5 balls ☐ p

10 yo-yos ☐ p   3 balls ☐ p

8 balls ☐ p   4 yo-yos ☐ p

2p

5p

How many yo-yos can you buy with 16p? ☐

How many balls can you buy with 20p? ☐

11 Colour red all the apples that have an answer in the two times table.

Colour green all the pears that have an answer in the five times table.

12 Complete these multiplications using the two and five times tables.

☐ × 5 = 25   ☐ × 2 = 12

☐ × 5 = 20   ☐ × 2 = 20

☐ × 5 = 40   ☐ × 2 = 10

☐ × 2 = 18   ☐ × 5 = 50

☐ × 5 = 5   ☐ × 2 = 8

Parent tip
Use the progress certificate at the back of this book to make a reward chart for your child.

How much did you do?   Questions 7–12

Circle the star to show what you have done.

 Some

 Most

 All

Mixed tables

Twos, fives and tens

1 Fill in the missing answers.

$4 \times 2 =$ ☐ $6 \times 2 =$ ☐ $4 \times 10 =$ ☐

$9 \times 5 =$ ☐ $10 \times 10 =$ ☐ $6 \times 5 =$ ☐

$3 \times 10 =$ ☐ $3 \times 5 =$ ☐ $9 \times 10 =$ ☐

$1 \times 5 =$ ☐ $10 \times 2 =$ ☐ $8 \times 2 =$ ☐

2 Look at these items.

How many flowers in 6 vases?   ☐ $\times$ ☐ $=$ ☐

How many socks in 8 pairs?   ☐ $\times$ ☐ $=$ ☐

How many candles on 4 cakes?   ☐ $\times$ ☐ $=$ ☐

I have 10 flowers. How many vases is this? ☐

I have 12 socks. How many pairs is this? ☐

There are 35 candles. How many cakes are there? ☐

3 Complete the multiplication grid.

×	2	5	8	1	9
2					
10					
5					

Parent tip
Find totals for piles of the same coin using 2p, 5p and 10p coins.

4 Look at the numbers in the box.
Draw a circle around any number that is an answer in the two times table.

Draw a square around any number that is an answer in the five times table.

Draw a triangle around any number that is an answer in the ten times table.

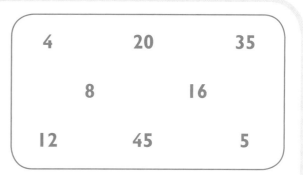

4	20	35
8	16
12	45	5

Which number is an answer in the two, five and ten times tables?

5 Work out the missing number to complete the multiplication on each safe. Find this number in the boxes below the safes. Write the letter from that safe in the box. What is the hidden word?

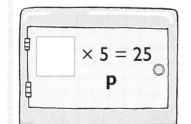
× 5 = 25
p

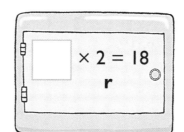
× 2 = 18
r

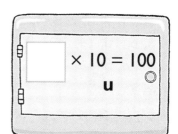
× 10 = 100
u

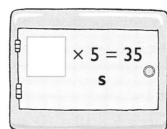
× 5 = 35
s

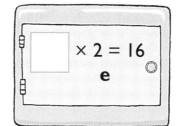
× 2 = 16
e

7	10	5	8	9	!

6 Write two different multiplications to give the answer in the middle of each bow.

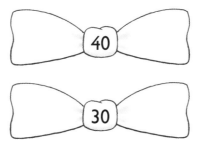

40

30

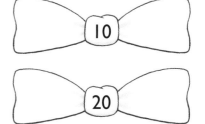

10

20

Answers

Two times table

Page 4

1 6, 14, 10, 12, 20, 4, 8, 16, 18
2 10, 6 × 2 = 12, 9 × 2 = 18
3 Colour 2, 6, 8, 10, 12, 14. It's a bird!

Page 5

4 Circle 8 × 2, 2 × 2, 5 × 2, 9 × 2
5 Colour red 16, 8, 10, 14, 2; colour blue 7, 13
6 8, 14, 18, 12

Page 6

7 7 × 2p = 14p; 5 × 2p = 10p; 9 × 2p = 18p; 6 × 2p = 12p
8 10, 5, 9, 8, 2, 3, 4, 1
9 6, 8, 10, 14, 16; 10, 12, 14, 16, 20; 16, 14, 12, 8, 6; 14, 12, 10, 4, 2

Page 7

10 ✔, ✔, ✗, ✗, ✗, ✔, ✗, ✔
11 Colour 2, 16, 4, 8, 20, 12, 6, 10, 14, 18
12 4 × 2 and 8; 6 × 2 and 12; 9 × 2 and 18; 2 × 2 and 4; 3 × 2 and 6; 10 × 2 and 20

Ten times table

Page 8

1 30, 60, 50, 90, 70, 80, 100, 20, 40
2 3 × 10p = 30p; 8 × 10p = 80p; 9 × 10p = 90p; 5 × 10p = 50p
3 50 and 5 × 10; 70 and 7 × 10; 100 and 10 × 10; 80 and 8 × 10; 10 and 1 × 10; 30 and 3 × 10

Page 9

4 30, 80, 90, 60
5 20, 40, 50, 60, 70; 90, 80, 60, 50, 40; 50, 60, 70, 80, 100; 60, 40, 30, 20, 10
6 5 × 10 = 50; 7 × 10 = 70; 9 × 10 = 90; 10 × 10 = 100

Page 10

7 Hat 80 = 8 × 10; bucket 60 = 6 × 10; football 70 = 7 × 10; bell 40 = 4 × 10; cup 10 = 1 × 10; book 50 = 5 × 10; clock 90 = 9 × 10
8 Circle 70, 50, 100, 40, 20

9 40, 10, 7, 10, 10, 3, 50, 20, 1, 8

Page 11

10 Colour 10, 40, 50, 70, 90. It's a guitar!
11 ✔, ✗, ✗, ✔, ✔, ✗, ✗, ✔, ✔
12 See inside front cover for the full ten times table

Mixed tables (twos and tens)

Page 12

1 4, 14, 12, 10, 30, 18, 100, 16, 60, 6, 50, 20, 2, 8, 10, 70, 20, 80, 40, 90
2 ×2 – 6, 12, 18, 20, 14; ×10 – 30, 60, 90, 100, 70
3 Circle green 2, 18, 10, 4, 12, 8, 20; circle red 10, 20; 10 and 20

Page 13

4 6 × 2 = 12, 6 × 10 = 60; 5 × 2 = 10, 5 × 10 = 50; 3 × 2 = 6, 3 × 10 = 30
5 Colour 8, 16, 20, 2, 100, 40
6 10 × 2 and 20; 8 × 2 and 16; 9 × 10 and 90; 7 × 2 and 14; 3 × 10 and 30; 5 × 10 and 50

Page 14

7 Circle 6 × 10 = 60; square 4 × 10 = 40; triangle 6 × 2 = 12; rectangle 8 × 2 = 16
8 12p, 30p, 8p, 50p, 16p, 70p
9 4 × 2 = pink; 1 × 10 and 5 × 2 = yellow; 7 × 2 = blue; 9 × 2 = green; 2 × 10 and 10 × 2 = red; 4 × 10 = purple

Page 15

10 4, 6, 10, 12, 14; 80, 60, 50, 40, 30; 18, 14, 12, 10, 8; 50, 60, 80, 90, 100
11 Start, 2, 90, 16, 40, 12, 70, 80, 30, 18, 50, 20, 14, 8, Finish
12 6, 2, 10, 6, 10, 10, 10, 4

Five times table

Page 16

1 15, 50, 25, 30, 35, 45, 20, 40, 10
2 It's an umbrella!
3 45 and 9 × 5; 15 and 3 × 5; 35 and 7 × 5; 25 and 5 × 5; 50 and 10 × 5

Page 17

4 Circle 4 × 5, 7 × 5, 3 × 5, 8 × 5

5 3 coins, 8 coins, 10 coins, 2 coins, 7 coins

6 ✔, ✔, ✗, ✔, ✔, ✗, ✗, ✗, ✔

Page 18

7 10, 15, 25, 30, 35; 40, 30, 25, 20, 15; 20, 25, 30, 40, 45; 30, 25, 20, 15, 5

8 Colour 5, 10, 15, 20, 25, 30, 35, 40, 45, 50

9 Colour 20, 30, 5, 50, 10, 15, 25

Page 19

10 door 50 = 10 × 5; moat 15 = 3 × 5; window 25 = 5 × 5; flag 20 = 4 × 5; drawbridge 35 = 7 × 5; wall 45 = 9 × 5; tower 5 = 1 × 5

11 9, 30, 2, 40, 4, 10

12 See inside front cover for the full five times table

Mixed tables (fives and tens)

Page 20

1 10, 80, 5, 40, 10, 35, 70, 40, 30, 60, 50, 45, 15, 100, 20, 25, 50, 20, 30, 90

2 2 × 5 and 1 × 10; 6 × 5 and 3 × 10; 4 × 5 and 2 × 10; 10 × 5 and 5 × 10; 8 × 5 and 4 × 10

3 Triangle 60 = 6 × 10; square 100 = 10 × 10; circle 25 = 5 × 5; oval 15 = 3 × 5; diamond 80 = 8 × 10; rectangle 45 = 9 × 5

Page 21

4 6 × 5p = 30p; 5 × 5p = 25p; 5 × 10p = 50p; 2 × 10p = 20p; 9 × 5p = 45p

5 ✔, ✗, ✗, ✔, ✔, ✗, ✗, ✔, ✗

6 15, 20, 25, 35; 20, 30, 35, 45; 40, 35, 30, 25, 15; 60, 50, 40, 20, 10; 20, 30, 50, 60, 70

Page 22

7 60, 30, 50, 90; 5, 45, 25, 35

8 Colour 10, 5, 25, 100, 50, 15, 80, 35, 45. It's the letter I!

9 25, 20, 7 × 5, 1 × 5, 10, 10 × 5 or 5 × 10, 30, 70, 10 × 10, 5 × 5

Page 23

10 ×5 – 10, 25, 35, 50, 40; ×10 – 20, 50, 70, 100, 80

11 Colour 5, 15, 35, 45, 50, 70, 80. It's a teapot!

12 (from top) 20, 15, 10, 90; (clockwise from top left) 10, 30, 7, 40, 10, 5, 5, 35

Mixed tables (twos and fives)

Page 24

1 6, 15, 2, 25, 5, 50, 20, 10, 35, 16, 14, 10, 8, 20, 18, 12, 45, 4, 30, 40, 20

2 10 × 2 and 20; 5 × 5 and 25; 8 × 5 and 40; 9 × 2 and 18; 7 × 5 and 35

3 5, 5, 10, 16, 8, 10, 20, 6

Page 25

4 Colour 2, 50, 35, 18, 12, 45

5 See inside front cover for the full two times table

6 6 × 2p = 12p; 6 × 5p = 30p; 3 × 5p = 15p; 3 × 2p = 6p

Page 26

7 6 × 5 = 30, 8 × 5 = 40, 4 × 5 = 20; 7 × 2 = 14, 5 × 2 = 10, 9 × 2 = 18

8 ✔, ✗, ✗, ✗, ✔, ✗, ✔, ✔, ✗

9 1 × 2 and 2; 5 × 5 and 25; 3 × 2 and 6; 2 × 5 and 10; 8 × 2 and 16

Page 27

10 12p, 25p, 20p, 15p, 40p, 8p; 8, 4

11 Colour red 2, 6, 12, 18; colour green 5, 15, 45, 50

12 5, 6, 4, 10, 8, 5, 9, 10, 1, 4

Mixed tables (twos, fives and tens)

Page 28

1 8, 12, 40, 45, 100, 30, 30, 15, 90, 5, 20, 16

2 6 × 10 = 60, 8 × 2 = 16, 4 × 5 = 20, 1, 6, 7

3 ×2 – 4, 10, 16, 2, 18; ×10 – 20, 50, 80, 10, 90; ×5 – 10, 25, 40, 5, 45

Page 29

4 Circle – 4, 20, 8, 16, 12; square – 20, 35, 45, 5; triangle – 20; 20 appears in all three

5 5, 9, 10, 7, 8; super!

6 10 × 4 and 8 × 5 = 40; 1 × 10 and 5 × 2 or 2 × 5 = 10; 3 × 10 and 6 × 5 = 30; 4 × 5 and 10 × 2 or 2 × 10 = 20

Check your progress

Did you find and colour all 14 monkeys?
(Including this one!)

- Shade in the stars on the progress certificate to show how much you did. Shade one star for every ⭐ you circled in this book.
- If you have shaded fewer than 10 stars go back to the pages where you circled Some ☆ or Most ⭐ and try those pages again.
- If you have shaded 10 or more stars you are ready to move on to the next workbook. Well done!

Collins Easy Learning Times Tables Age 5–7 Workbook 1

Progress certificate

to _____

name _____

date _____

Two		Ten		Twos and tens		Five		Fives and tens		Twos and fives		Twos, fives and tens
pages 4–5	pages 6–7	pages 8–9	pages 10–11	pages 12–13	pages 14–15	pages 16–17	pages 18–19	pages 20–21	pages 22–23	pages 24–25	pages 26–27	pages 28–29
1	2	3	4	5	6	7	8	9	10	11	12	13